The COLLEGE FOOTBALL Hall of Fame

A chronicle of the game's history and America's premiere sports museum

by **Kent Stephens**

Copyright © 2000 by The College Football Hall of Fame

All photographs courtesy The College Football Hall of Fame unless noted.

All rights reserved, including the right to reproduce this work in any form whatsoever without permission in writing from the publisher, except for brief passages in connection with a review.

For information, write:

The Donning Company Publishers
184 Business Park Drive, Suite 106
Virginia Beach, VA 23462

Steve Mull, General Manager
Ed Williams, Project Director
Debbie Williams, Project Research Coordinator
Dawn V. Kofroth, Assistant General Manager
Sally Clarke Davis, Editor
Marshall Rouse McClure, Graphic Designer
John Harrell, Imaging Artist
Scott Rule, Marketing Coordinator

Library of Congress Cataloging-in-Publication Data

AVAILABLE UPON REQUEST

Printed in the United States of America

Contents

CHAPTER I
The National Football Foundation 5

CHAPTER II
History of College Football 7

How the Game Began • 7
American Innovations • 10
The Game is Saved • 13
New Strategies • 16
Football's Roaring Twenties • 19
Bowls and Polls • 24
The War Years • 27
The Fabulous Fifties • 31
Games of the Century • 35
Run to Daylight • 38
Bombs Away • 41
Who's Number One • 44

CHAPTER III
The Museum....................51

How the Museum Was Built • 51
Great Rivals • 52
Covering the Game • 53
Fields, Footballs and Officials • 54
Scholar-Athletes • 55
Evolution of the Equipment • 56
Pigskin Pageantry • 58
Bowl Games • 59
National Champions • 60
Pantheon • 61
Hall of Honor • 62
How One Becomes a Hall of Famer • 63

ABOUT THE AUTHOR 64

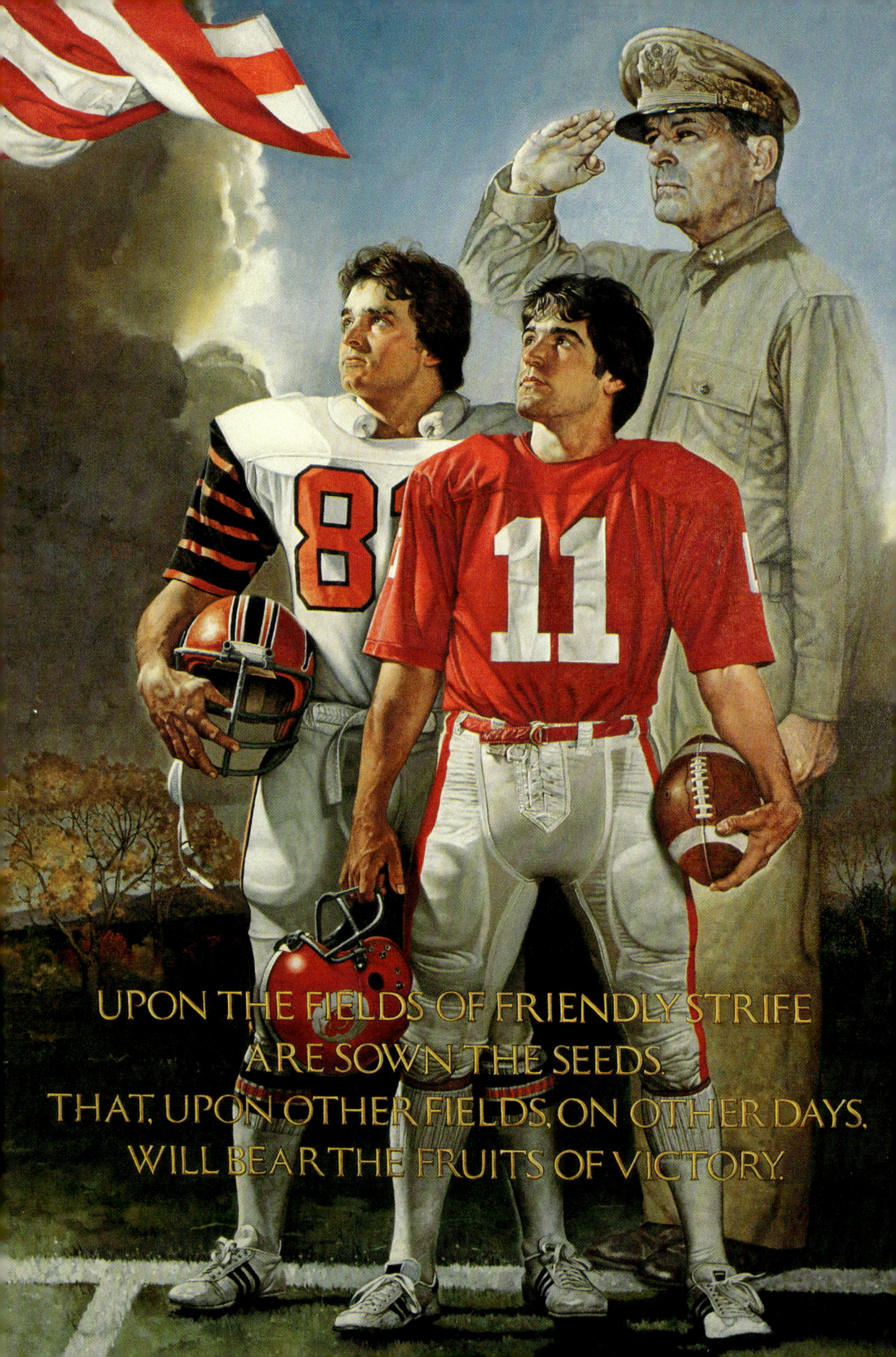

CHAPTER I

The National Football Foundation

With legendary sportswriter Grantland Rice as one of its founding members, the National Football Foundation was originated in 1947. The NFF's purpose is to mobilize the constructive forces of amateur football for the benefit of the country and give permanence to the history of the game.

It accomplishes that goal through many programs. The NFF is supported by over ten thousand members in more than a hundred local chapters throughout the nation. On the local level, the NFF annually honors over three thousand high school football players for their excellence on the field, in the classroom, and in the community. Nationally, the Foundation honors collegiate scholar-athletes and combines with the chapters to annually award nearly a million dollars in scholarships.

On both the local and national level, the NFF also honors those who have excelled on and off the field and have demonstrated the Foundation's creed of scholarship, citizenship, and athletic performance.

To preserve the game's history the foundation began electing players and coaches to the Hall of Fame in 1951, with an inaugural class of fifty-four players and coaches. The Foundation has held annual elections since 1954. The Foundation first built a home to honor these great men and achievements in 1978, with the Hall of Fame relocating to South Bend in 1995. • • •

Created for the National Football Foundation during college football's centennial season of 1969, this painting is displayed at the Hall of Fame in the National Champions exhibit. The painting depicts General Douglas MacArthur and the captains of the Rutgers and Princeton teams.

Early American football was strictly a kicking game that was played between any number of players.

CHAPTER II

History of College Football

How the Game Began

The game of football may be the most elementary of all games. In its simplest form, football involves moving an object across a specified distance into a goal defended by an opposing team or group.

Cavemen most likely played games utilizing this basic concept. One of the first football-like games known to have a set of codified rules was the Greek game of Harpaston. The game called for a rectangular field marked by a center line and goal lines at the ends of the field. The rules stipulated that a leather ball stuffed with hair or wool, could only be advanced by kicking. The game probably was introduced to England at the time of the Roman Empire.

During the middle ages football was so popular in Britain that it had to survive royal attempts to make

The Greek game of Harpaston was one of the first "football games" to have a set of codified rules. The game's name comes from a Greek verb which means to seize. Most feel that tackling probably was permissible

Kicking was the only way of advancing the ball until late in a scoreless game at the Rugby School when William Webb Ellis changed the course of sports history.

the game illegal. All manners of this kicking game were played during these times. In 1823, one play changed the course of sport history. Near the end of a match at the Rugby School, William Webb Ellis broke the rules by catching the ball and running toward the goal. From this unprecedented act saw the development of an entirely new game called Rugby.

From this time on there were two football games. In Rugby it was permissible to carry the ball, in the other the ball was kicked. Both games continued to develop with the kicking game often being referred to as Association football, from which the term soccer was derived.

In America, colleges and universities began playing football in

The English game of football was often a series of undisciplined matches that pitted one class against another. Not until inter-school matches were played did codified rules result.

intramural competitions. Most of these contests were played without established rules or organization.

In 1869, Princeton challenged Rutgers to the first intercollegiate football game. The rules of this match specified that the game be played between 25-man teams, the ball was to be kicked or butted with the head, carrying was prohibited, and the first team to score six goals would be declared the winner. On November 6, at Rutgers University Field, Rutgers prevailed 6–4. A week later the two teams met again with Princeton winning 8–0. College football was born. • • •

On Nov. 25, 1869, Rutgers met Princeton in the first intercollegiate football game. The Rutgers players wore red scarves to distinguish themselves from the Princeton players, giving future Rutgers teams the nickname of Scarlet Knights. ARNOLD FRIBERG

American Innovations

The first game did not inspire a meteoric growth of intercollegiate football. Columbia joined Princeton and Rutgers by playing one game in 1870, with no intercollegiate games being played the following year.

In 1873, the first formal rules were adopted. The rules specified that football was to be a kicking game. Seven schools fielded teams.

Harvard played a series of three games with McGill University of Montreal, Canada the next season. McGill played rugby while Harvard played a game more like soccer. In the second of their three games, the teams agreed to play under modified rules of the Rugby Football Union.

The new running game was met with great enthusiasm and was

In a 1879 Princeton-Yale game, the backs wait for the ball to be kicked out of the scrum in a match played under rugby-like rules.

Walter Camp is known as the "Father of American Football." He played and coached at Yale and was the creative force behind many rule innovations that made American football a unique sport. YALE UNIVERSITY

Pudge Heffelfinger of Yale was a member of the first All-America team selected in 1889. He is regarded as one of the greatest guards to have ever played the game. YALE UNIVERSITY

adopted by Harvard, Yale, Princeton, and Columbia. In 1876, representatives from these four schools met in Springfield, Massachusetts to develop a set of rules for a running game and form an Intercollegiate Football Association.

Over the next five years, the number of schools that fielded teams exceeded twenty.

In 1880, football finally became a contest that resembled today's game. Walter Camp of Yale was able to persuade the rules committee to adopt a number of his innovations. Most importantly was his concept of ball possession through the introduction of the scrimmage line. Having one team clearly possessing the ball allowed for strategic and tactical preparation both offensively and defensively.

Two years later, Camp introduced the concept of down and distance, where a team had to gain five yards in three plays to maintain possession.

Throughout the 1880s, college football continued to grow. By the end of the decade over seventy schools fielded teams. And while the sport was still an eastern game, football was being played in isolated spots in the Midwest, South, and West.

The national media began to take increasing notice, and in 1889, Caspar Whitney of *The Week's Sport* collaborated with Camp to select the first All-America team.

The rules and tactics of the late nineteenth century football made for an extremely brutal game. The players on the line stood shoulder to shoulder as the backs were pushed and pulled between the tackles in plays of mass momentum to gain the short yardage necessary to maintain possession of the ball.

As there were no restrictions as to the number of men that had to be placed on the line of scrimmage, offenses put linemen into the backfield to help run interference on the mass-momentum plays.

The game became increasingly brutal, and as the injuries and deaths escalated, many began to call for the abolishment of the sport. • • •

TOP: *This 1891 illustration contributed to the public's outcry against the brutality of college football.*

ABOVE: *The flying wedge was the most brutal of all nineteenth century plays. Players would lock arms or join together by holding on each other's belt while protecting the ball carrier in the middle of the V.* BETTMAN ARCHIVES

The Game is Saved

At the turn of the twentieth century, football had spread throughout the nation.

While the game's core was still in the East, the rest of the country was making inroads as non-eastern players were increasingly found on All-America lists and a select few non-eastern teams were considered as equals to the more established teams.

The game's growing popularity in the last decade of the nineteenth century made the game a more sophisticated economic enterprise, which led to a near universal use of professional coaches, a rarely found occurrence only a decade before.

Proof of the economic potential of football was that the University of Michigan was invited west to participate in a game as part of the Tournament of Roses Festival in Pasadena, California. The 8,500 spectators at the first Rose Bowl game easily exceeded the 1,000-seat stadium capacity.

Football was still a game of mass momentum. All of the brutal and unsportsmanlike elements that had become all too commonplace such as punching, gouging,

The first Rose Bowl was played to an overflow crowd. Michigan's dominance over Stanford led both parties to agree to end the game with eight minutes remaining to be played.
TOURNAMENT OF ROSES

and piling-on continued.

The rough play peaked in 1905, when 18 players died and over 150 more were seriously injured. University presidents began wondering if the game was worth the carnage. Universities either dropped, or were threatening to abolish the sport.

President Theodore Roosevelt called for representatives of Harvard, Princeton, and Yale to meet with him at the White House. Roosevelt supported the game and asked that these men take the lead to change the rules before football was universally abolished.

In a January 1906 meeting, the game's rules makers made significant changes to eliminate rough play and save the game's future.

To eliminate brutal play, the rules makers sought to open up the

KILLED IN A FOOTBALL GAME.

John C. Dondero Dead and His Brother Will Lose an Eye.

WILLIMANTIC, Conn., Oct. 22.—John C. Dondero, 27 years old, died to-day as the result of an injury received in a football game in Jewett City.

Dondero was a member of the Willimantic team, and it is said that he was in no condition to play. After a scrimmage he lay on the field unconscious and was taken to a hotel, where he died. Doctors state that a cerebral hemorrhage was the cause of his death, superinduced by the player's poor physical condition at the time of the game.

A brother of Dondero was kicked in the eye in the same game, and will lose the eye.

Headlines such as this were common during the tragic 1905 season. NEW YORK TIMES

President Theodore Roosevelt was hailed by many as the savior of college football. Roosevelt's own son was a victim of rough play as Theodore Jr. was injured while playing for the Harvard freshmen. NEW YORK TIMES

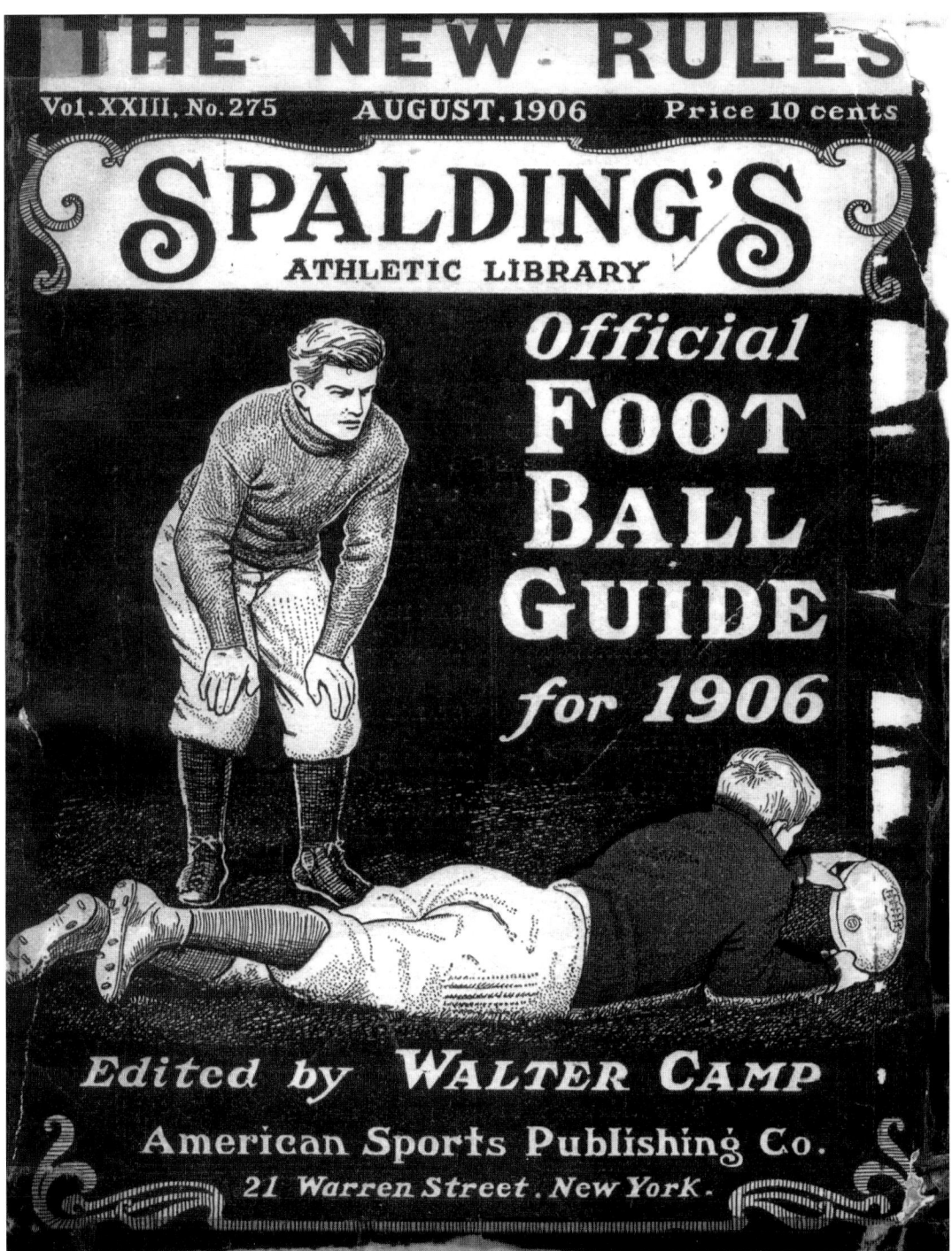

Guide books for the 1906 season prominently featured the new rules. A.G. SPALDING

game by implementing several significant changes. Most important were the legalization of the forward pass, the creation of the neutral zone between the opposing lines, and increasing the number of yards necessary to gain a first down from five to ten yards. • • •

w Strategies

The rule changes of 1906 did not result in immediate and drastic changes in the way the game was played. Most coaches continued with mass momentum plays and were slow to adopt the use of the forward pass. As a result, deaths and serious injuries were still a part of the game.

The first team to use the pass and one of the few teams that utilized the pass as a regular part of their offense was St. Louis University.

In 1910, another attempt to rid the game of mass play and brutality was made by eliminating the aiding of a runner's progress by pushing and pulling, and requiring seven men on the line of scrimmage. Two years later, the field was shortened to one hundred yards, end zones were added, and the number of plays per series of downs was increased from three to four.

Before 1910, there were few

The Notre Dame passing combination of Knute Rockne (left) and Gus Dorais (right) was formed during the summer months as the two practiced along the shore of Lake Erie while they were lifeguards at Cedar Point amusement park.
UNIVERSITY OF NOTRE DAME

Glenn "Pop" Warner (far right) poses with three of his Carlisle players including Hall of Fame member Albert Exendine (second from the right).

intrasectional games. Improved transportation made these interesting match-ups more commonplace. One intrasectional game would play a major role in the development of the pass.

In 1913, Notre Dame traveled east to play a favored Army team. In completing 14 of 17 passes, Notre Dame quarterback Gus Dorais and end Knute Rockne helped to upset the Cadets 35–13. The passing display legitimized the pass and proved to eastern powers that the forward pass could be an effective offensive strategy.

The accumulated effect of six years of rule changes from 1906–1912 finally began to result in real change to open up the game. Carlisle Coach "Pop" Warner was at the forefront of these strategic changes with his invention of both the single and double wing formations.

"We needed something that would take care of both the running game and the new forward pass. The single wing gave an offense the chance for deception that it hadn't had before," explained Warner.

Jim Thorpe (back row far right) played at Carlisle from 1907–1908 and 1911–1912. In his senior year, Thorpe scored twenty-nine touchdowns. CUMBERLAND COUNTY HISTORICAL SOCIETY

Coach John Heisman led Georgia Tech in a record setting 222–0 victory over Cumberland College in 1916. GEORGIA TECH ATHLETIC ASSOCIATION

His formations spurred the development of new plays that utilized deception and faking rather than power. Plays such as spinners, reverses, and fake reverses were now possible.

Other coaches contributed to the offensive revolution with the development of the short punt, spread, and Y formations.

While at the Carlisle Indian Industrial School, Warner coached the legendary Jim Thorpe. There were better teams, but Thorpe and his teammates were perhaps the most colorful and exciting team of their era. Thorpe was the perfect player who combined speed, power, and elusiveness. An Olympic gold medal winner and major league baseball player, Thorpe was voted as the greatest overall athlete and football player of the first half of the twentieth century. • • •

RIGHT: The famous "Four Horsemen" photograph was the idea of Notre Dame student publicist George Strickler who arranged to have the Notre Dame backfield pose on horses delivered to the practice field. UNIVERSITY OF NOTRE DAME

Football's Roaring Twenties

College football may have experienced its greatest growth in popularity during the 1920s. The advent and popularization of radio and motion pictures technologies, along with the support of sportswriters such as Grantland Rice, Paul Gallico, Ring Lardner, and Damon Runyon helped the game take its place in the "Golden Era of Sports."

The previously mentioned media had many stars and personalities to cover.

The most prominent coach of the decade was Notre Dame's Knute Rockne. His personality and his team's exciting and wide-open style of play produced a career record of 105–12–5, making the Fighting Irish the nation's most popular team.

One of his greatest teams was his first national championship squad of 1924. On October 18 of that year, Grantland Rice covered the Notre Dame-Army game and dubbed the Notre Dame backfield, "The Four Horsemen" in the most remembered lead in sportswriting history.

On the same day that Rice was

Knute Rockne's winning percentage of .881 tops all major college coaches. UNIVERSITY OF NOTRE DAME

Harold "Red" Grange was an elusive runner with great balance and vision. His trademark runs often came in the shape of an S as he reversed his field from sideline to sideline. UNIVERSITY OF ILLINOIS

witnessing the Four Horsemen, eight hundred miles to the west, Red Grange of Illinois had one of the greatest individual days in the game's history. Against Michigan, he scored four touchdowns in the game's first twelve minutes on runs of 95, 67, 56, and 44 yards.

Only Grange rivaled Rockne's celebrity, as "The Galloping Ghost" was to college football in the 1920s what Babe Ruth was to baseball, or Jack Dempsey to boxing.

Rockne was a master psychologist and motivator of players through his inspiring halftime talks. At halftime of the 1928 Army game, Rockne told his players the story of George Gipp. Pneumonia claimed Rockne's greatest player eight years previously. While on his death bed, the 23-year old Gipp made a plea to Rockne that, "when the team's up against it, when things are going wrong and the breaks are beating the boys, tell them to go in there with all they've got and win just one for the Gipper."

The 77 jersey Grange wore is on display in the Hall of Fame 1920s section of the Hall of Champions.

Bo McMillin led Centre's Praying Colonels to a victory over Harvard in 1921, handing the Crimson their first varsity defeat since 1916. Jubilant Centre students painted "C-6 H-0" on the school's administration building. CENTRE COLLEGE

Inspired by the tale of Gipp's deathbed wish, Notre Dame rallied in the second half to upset Army.

The powers of college football were now no longer centered in the east. Each section of the country produced great players and teams. From the West, California's "Wonder Teams" had a 46-0-4 record from 1920-1924.

The south gained prominence in 1921 when tiny Centre College of Danville, Kentucky upset Harvard 6-0. Later in the decade, Alabama won back-to-back national titles in 1925 and 1926.

The popularity of football in the 1920s was reflected in a stadium building boom, as numerous structures exceeding 60,000 seating capacities were built. Some of the largest crowds in football history were recorded in the 1920s as the 110,000 spectator mark was exceeded four times at Chicago's Soldier Field. • • •

FACING PAGE:
The 1926 dedication game of Chicago's Soldier Field saw Navy rally to tie Army 21-21 and preserve their national championship in front of 110,000 people.

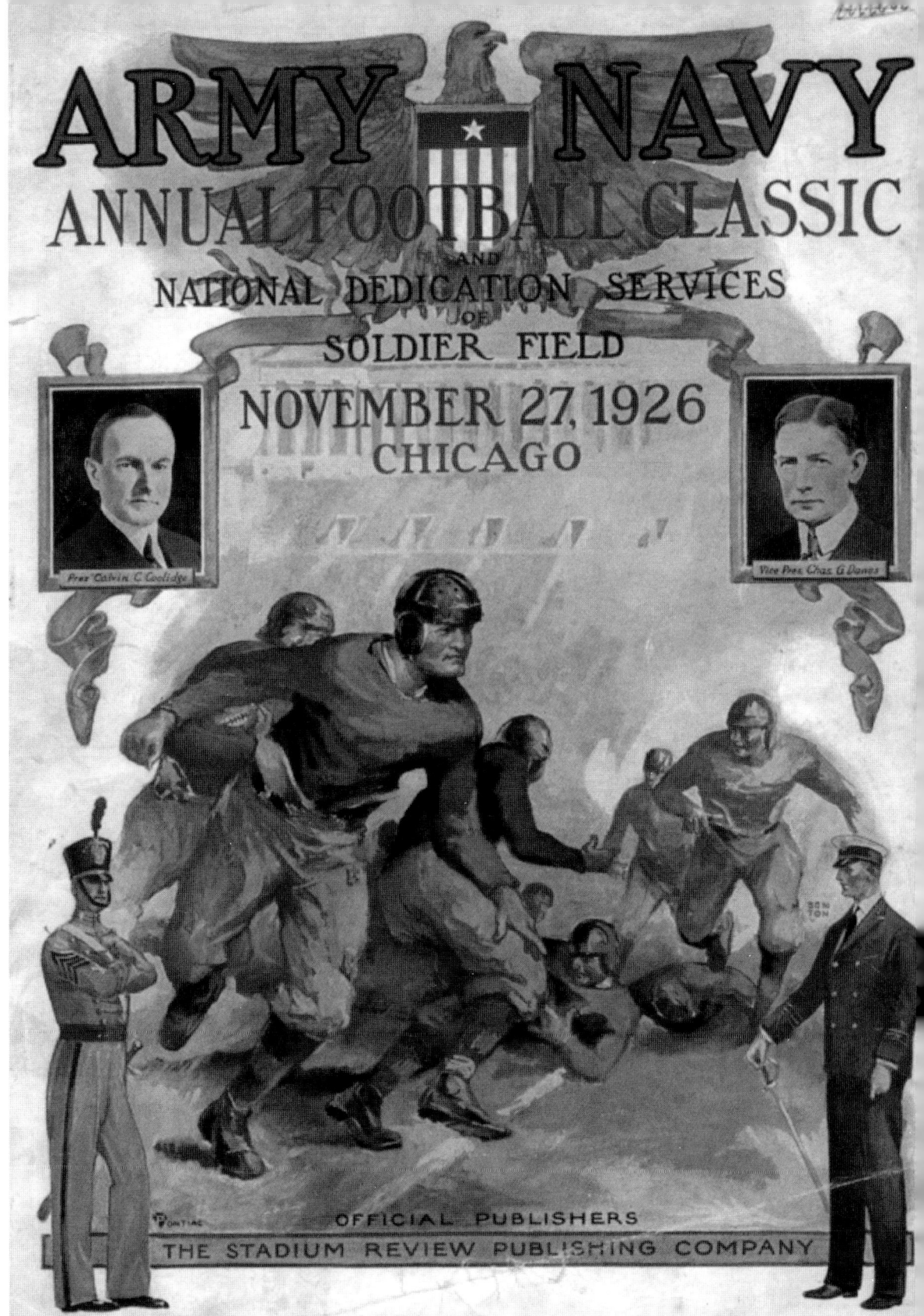

ABOVE: Sammy Baugh was one of the first players to take advantage of the new streamlined ball. His passes were not enough to defeat Southern Methodist in a game that decided the national championship of 1935. TEXAS CHRISTIAN UNIVERSITY

Bowls and Polls

Despite the severe blow dealt to college football at the start of the decade on March 31, 1931 when Knute Rockne died in a plane crash, college football continued to prosper, develop, and change.

Football has always been known as "a game of inches." This tiny measurement made a significant difference in 1934, when the circumference of the ball was reduced an inch. The streamlining of the ball made it easier to throw and further

BELOW: Chicago's Jay Berwanger was not only the first Heisman Trophy winner, but was the first player selected in the inaugural NFL draft. UNIVERSITY OF CHICAGO

opened up the passing game.

Teams in the Southwest Conference were among the first to take advantage of the new equipment. At Texas Christian they produced the two greatest passers of the era in Sammy Baugh and Davey O'Brien.

As the nation was in the midst of the Depression, communities were looking for additional means of economic development. A series of benefit games were played in the early thirties. Midway through the decade, the cities of Miami, New Orleans, El Paso, and Dallas utilized college football as a way to attract tourists with the beginning of the Orange, Sugar, Sun, and Cotton Bowls.

Another mid-thirties innovation was the awarding of the Heisman Trophy, the first major individual college football award. Jay Berwanger of Chicago won the inaugural Heisman in 1935.

Weekly polls were instituted during the thirties with the beginning of the Associated Press Top 20.

The decade produced many colorful team nicknames. Fordham's famed line was dubbed, "The Seven Blocks of Granite." Howard Jones' Southern California teams were known as "The Thundering Herd." The backfield of Goldberg,

Berwanger's helmet was one of the first to contain a face mask. The mask was designed by the Chicago trainer after Berwanger was injured in a freshman game. He was often called, "The Man in the Iron Mask."

Fordham's "Seven Blocks of Granite" were anchored by Hall of Famer Alex Wojciechowicz (center) and featured Vince Lombardi (third from the left).
FORDHAM UNIVERSITY

Unlike Rockne, Minnesota's Bernie Bierman did not whip his players into an emotional state. Bierman believed a calm and determined team was more effective.
UNIVERSITY OF MINNESOTA

Stebbins, Cassiano, and Chickerneo were called Pittsburgh's "Dream Backfield." At Stanford, a group of freshmen known as the "Vow Boys" kept a pledge to never lose to Southern California.

Perhaps the dominant team of the decade was Bernie Bierman's Minnesota Golden Gophers who won five national championships between 1934 and 1941.

The greatest game of the decade occurred in 1935 when undefeated Ohio State hosted undefeated Notre Dame. Known as the "Scarlet Scourge," Francis Schmidt's Buckeyes led 13–0 going into the fourth quarter. The Irish scored twice but missed both extra point attempts to trail 13–12. With fifty-five seconds to play, Ohio State fumbled at mid-field setting up a last-second 20-yard Notre Dame touchdown pass to win 18–13. Many historians still rate this contest as the greatest game ever played. • • •

The War Years

The decade of the forties is one of college football's most interesting eras. Several developments changed the way the game was played, and the overall quality of play during the post war era may have been the game's high-water mark.

The decade began with Stanford's Clark Shaughnessy abandoning the single-wing offense for the T formation. The revolutionary style of offense prompted Pop Warner to remark, "If Stanford wins a single game with that formation, you can throw everything I know about football into the Pacific Ocean."

The Stanford season of 1940 is one of the most remarkable in history as Shaughnessy turned a 1–7–1 team in 1939 into a 10–0 Rose Bowl champion team. At the time, the transformation was the greatest single-season improvement in college football history.

Like the rest of the nation, World War II had a great impact upon the game. The January 1, 1942 Rose Bowl was moved from Pasadena to Durham, North Carolina in fear of a Japanese attack one month after the bombing of Pearl Harbor. With a lack of players, 305 schools dropped the sport during the war. To make up for the overall lack of personnel, rule makers allowed for free substitution. This change would have its greatest impact after the war.

As the University of Chicago's head coach, Clark Shaughnessy also was an advisor to the Chicago Bears. He helped the Bears install the T formation before he went to Stanford. STANFORD UNIVERSITY

Fullback Doc Blanchard, Coach Earl Blaik and halfback Glenn Davis (left to right) were part of an Army team that had a 27–0–1 record from 1944–1946. UNITED STATES MILITARY ACADEMY

As many players were in the various branches of the military, college teams scheduled games against service teams. Most of these teams were stocked with former collegiate and professional players. In the final Top 20 poll of 1944, ten of the teams listed were service teams.

During the war, Army was easily the nation's most powerful team. In winning national titles in both 1944 and 1945, the Cadets had only two games where victory was by a margin of less than twenty points.

The jersey worn by 1946 Heisman Trophy winner Glenn Davis is located in the 1940s area of the Hall of Champions.

The key play of the 1946 Army-Notre Dame game came when the Notre Dame's John Lujack saved a touchdown with a tackle of Doc Blanchard. WORLD WIDE PHOTO

Army featured the game's greatest backfield duo of Doc Blanchard and Glenn Davis, "Mr. Inside and Mr. Outside," the 1945 and 1946 Heisman Trophy winners.

After the war, college teams experienced a glut of talent as war-toughened veterans returned to the campus to compete for playing time with existing players.

One team that benefited from the return of veterans was Notre Dame, which entered the 1946 Army game undefeated. The clash of unbeaten

No. 1 and No. 2 teams was probably the most anticipated game in college history. Despite the numerous stars, All-America and Heisman Trophy winning players on both teams, the contest ended in a 0–0 tie.

The rest of the decade was dominated by Notre Dame and Michigan. Michigan head coach Fritz Crisler took advantage of the free substitution rule change by creating separate offensive and defensive platoons. The Wolverines won twenty-five consecutive games between 1946–1949, while Notre Dame under Frank Leahy was 36–0–2 during the same time period. • • •

Michigan coach Fritz Crisler celebrates a victory over Wisconsin with Bruce Hilene and future Hall of Famers, Bump (18) and Pete Elliott (45).
UNIVERSITY OF MICHIGAN

The Fabulous Fifties

Free substitution and two-platoon football continued until 1953 when the rules reverted to pre-war standards. Once again a player had to be a multi-talented, versatile, well-conditioned athlete who had to play on both offense and defense, often for sixty minutes.

The type of football played in the 1950s was extremely diverse. Many teams such as UCLA and Tennessee still used the old single-wing, while other teams began developing variations off Shaughnessy's T formation.

Forest Evashevski of Iowa was one of the principal developers of the winged-T formation, while Bud Wilkinson of Oklahoma perfected the split-T introduced by Don Faurot of Missouri.

Bud Wilkinson played for Minnesota's Bernie Bierman and learned the split-T as an assistant to Don Faurot while in the military. Oklahoma's remarkable 47-game win streak was bookended by losses to Notre Dame in 1953 and 1957.
UNIVERSITY OF OKLAHOMA

Wilkinson and his Sooners would dominate the decade. From 1950–1959 his teams compiled a 93–10–2 record that included a forty-seven game win-streak and three national championships.

The advent of television was a major concern to college football in the 1950s. Over time it was found that instead of decreasing gate attendance, television helped develop an interest in the sport with the casual fan and created greater awareness of the sport.

The advent of television helped give a nickname to the 1955 Heisman Trophy winner Howard Cassady of Ohio State. Assuming the name of a popular television cowboy of the time,

The Chinese Bandits held opposing runners to less than a yard a carry. LOUISIANA STATE UNIVERSITY

In the 1954 Cotton Bowl, Dick Maegle of Rice (with ball) was tackled when Alabama's Tommy Lewis (42) came off the bench to bring Maegle down along the sidelines. COTTON BOWL

the Buckeye halfback was forever known as "Hopalong Cassady."

One of the most colorful teams of the era was the Louisiana State Tigers of 1958. In winning the national championship that season, Coach Paul Dietzel created three separate teams. His regular group was known as the "White Team." On occasion he would utilize an offensive platoon known as the "Go Team" or a defensive unit known as "The Chinese Bandits." Dietzel was able to utilize these three separate platoons while still playing under the rules of one-platoon football.

The 1950s were the final hurrah of football's founding teams of Yale,

Syracuse's Ernie Davis helped lead the Orangemen to the 1959 National Championship. Two years later, Davis would become the first African-American to win the Heisman Trophy. Davis died of leukemia before he had an opportunity to play professionally. SYRACUSE UNIVERSITY

Harvard, and Princeton as major powers. The No. 6 ranking of Princeton in 1951 would mark the final time an Ivy League team would appear among the nation's top ten teams.

That same year the National Football Foundation elected its first class of inductees to the College Football Hall of Fame. In 1958, the Foundation held its first annual awards dinner. • • •

Games of the Century

Until the 1960s, meetings of the nation's top two teams were rare occurrences. The last such meeting was in 1946. During the sixties there were seven No. 1 vs. No. 2 match-ups. Most of the games were exciting late season or bowl contests that would determine the national championship.

The 1963 Rose Bowl game between Southern California and Wisconsin started out to be anything but forgettable. The Trojans led 42–14 early in the fourth quarter. But behind Badger quarterback Ron VanderKellen, Wisconsin made a remarkable comeback closing the score to 42–37 when time finally ran out on the Badgers.

Perhaps the only game in college history that was greeted with as much anticipation as the Army-Notre Dame game of 1946 happened twenty years later when Michigan State hosted Notre Dame.

The result was much the same as the 1946 game as two star-laden teams battled to an exciting, yet inconclusive and disappointing 10–10 tie.

The final No. 1 vs. No. 2 game of the decade came in 1969 when Texas met Arkansas. With President Nixon in the stands, the Longhorns rallied from a 14–0 fourth quarter deficit to defeat the Razorbacks and accept a plaque from the President as the nation's top team.

There were many never to be forgotten games that were played

TOP: In the early going of the 1963 Rose Bowl, Willie Brown and his Southern California teammates were running away from Wisconsin. TOURNAMENT OF ROSES

ABOVE: The 1963 Navy backfield featured quarterback Roger Staubach (12). The Midshipmen were the nation's second-ranked team, the last time a service academy finished among the nation's top ten teams. UNITED STATES NAVAL ACADEMY

The 1966 match-up between Michigan State and Notre Dame featured sixteen players who would gain All-America notice that season. UNIVERSITY OF NOTRE DAME

during the sixties. In 1967, top ranked UCLA led by Gary Beban met Southern California, led by O.J. Simpson. The game determined the championship of Los Angeles, the conference crown, perhaps the national title, and the Heisman Trophy. The Trojans won the game 21–20 on a 64-yard run by Simpson.

Two years later when Michigan upset Ohio State 24–12, it ended a 22-game winning streak of a team many considered to be the decade's best, and began a ten-year rivalry between Ohio State Coach Woody

UCLA's Gary Beban lost against Southern California in 1967, but gained enough support to claim that year's Heisman Trophy. UNIVERSITY OF CALIFORNIA AT LOS ANGELES

Hayes and his former assistant, Michigan's Bo Schembechler.

Midway thorough the decade, substitution rules were changed again to allow for free substitution and two-platoon football. Platoon football allowed for specialization of talents. The impact was most noticeable on offense as the number of pass plays per game increased from 31 in 1960, to 51 in 1969, while the number of total plays per game increased from 122 to 150.

While passing was increasing, an offensive development late in the decade would affect the ratio of run to pass for the 1970s. In 1968, Darrell Royal of Texas introduced the Wishbone offense. The formation got its unusual name because of the positioning of the players in the backfield. This option offense was run dominated and would become one of the fashionable attacks of the 1970s. • • •

Texas quarterback James Street confers with Coach Darrell Royal during a critical point in the 1970 Cotton Bowl. Texas gained a first down, scored, and defeated Notre Dame in the Irish's first bowl appearance since 1925. COTTON BOWL

Run to Daylight

Since its beginning, college football had always been a stratified sport between major and minor teams or big school and small college teams. In the seventies, this stratification was formalized as teams were divided into various divisions with separate awards, playoffs, and championships for each division.

The influence of the wishbone formation and the I formation made college football increasingly run dominated. At the decade's mid-point there were three running plays for every pass play where just five years previously the ratio was two running plays for every pass.

As a consequence, many all-time rushing records would fall. In 1971, Cornell's Ed Marinaro would surpass the all-time career mark of Oklahoma's Steve Owens by nearly 800 yards. Four years later Archie Griffin would take over as the game's all-time rusher. He would hold the crown for only a season as his mark was smashed by over 900 yards by Pittsburgh's Tony Dorsett.

In addition to winning two Heisman trophies, Archie Griffin was the first player to start in four Rose Bowls. OHIO STATE UNIVERSITY

Griffin's jersey is on display in the 1970s area of the Hall of Champions.

Both Griffin and Dorsett would win the Heisman Trophy, with Griffin becoming the only two-time winner of the award. When John Cappelletti of Penn State won the Heisman in 1973, it began an eleven year run where only running backs would claim the trophy.

In addition to winning the 1976 Heisman Trophy, Tony Dorsett led Pittsburgh to an undefeated season and the national championship. UNIVERSITY OF PITTSBURGH

Cappelletti's acceptance is one of the most memorable speeches in all of sports when he tearfully dedicated the trophy to his eleven-year-old brother who was battling leukemia. Joey would die in 1976.

As running the football would be the principal strategy of the day, two wishbone teams would find themselves as the era's best teams. Oklahoma would win two national titles, have a 28-game win streak and have a decade's best record of 102–13–3 with backfield stars such as Billy Sims and Joe Washington.

Coach Bear Bryant's Alabama's Crimson Tide would not be far behind the Sooners with a 103–16–1 record, and three national titles.

The most memorable of these titles came in 1978 when the Tide defense made a memorable goal line stand against Penn State in the 1979 Sugar Bowl to preserve a 14–7 victory.

John Cappelletti gave perhaps the most moving of all Heisman Trophy acceptance speeches when he dedicated the trophy to his critically ill brother. President Gerald Ford is standing at the far right. DOWNTOWN ATHLETIC CLUB

Johnny Rodgers opened the scoring in the 1971 clash with Oklahoma with a first-quarter punt return. Rodgers would later make a critical first down catch on the game clinching touchdown drive late in the fourth quarter.
UNIVERSITY OF NEBRASKA

The biggest game of the decade may also have been the most exciting game ever played. Top-ranked Nebraska met second ranked Oklahoma on Thanksgiving Day of 1971. Nebraska took the lead on a 72-yard punt return by Johnny Rodgers. Twice behind by eleven points, Oklahoma continually battled back behind quarterback Jack Mildren. Late in the game, Nebraska went on a 74-yard drive to claim a 35–31 victory. • • •

On a day that featured freezing rain, Notre Dame quarterback Joe Montana ate chicken soup from this bowl allowing him to raise his body temperature and lead Notre Dame to a last minute 35–34 victory in the Cotton Bowl.

Bombs Away

The move to divisional play in the 1970s produced a number of small college dynasties in the 1980s. In Division I-AA, Georgia Southern won four national championships between 1985 and 1990. North Dakota State won five championships from 1983–1990 in Division II, and Augustana dominated Division III by taking four consecutive titles starting in 1983. On the NAIA level, Carson-Newman won five championships, while Linfield took three.

During the 1980s, the style of play would change again. The natural order of football seems to be that as one aspect of the game dominates play, new strategies are developed to neutralize the old strategy. In the 1980s, defenses caught up to the running game of the seventies, while the rule makers gave a helping hand to the passing game.

The committee members liberalized pass blocking techniques, enabling the pass completion percentages in 1980 to exceed 50 percent for the first time in history. And in 1982, total passing yardage would overtake rushing yardage for the first time. The increased passing also led to higher scoring games and a number of exciting last minute heroics.

The 1980 Holiday Bowl was a

Augustana won their first of four consecutive national championships by defeating Union 21–17.

41

wild, high scoring game that ended with Jim McMahon completing a last second 50-yard touchdown bomb that gave Brigham Young a 46–45 victory over Southern Methodist.

Four years later, Doug Flutie of Boston College also threw a last-second 50-yard touchdown pass that beat Miami. The nationally televised day after Thanksgiving game in the Orange Bowl Stadium clinched the Heisman Trophy for Flutie.

The Orange Bowl was the site of numerous big games during the eighties. The previous season, Miami beat Nebraska 31–30 in a national championship contest when the Cornhuskers failed on a last-minute, two-point conversion. Three other national titles would be decided in the Orange Bowl during the eighties.

TOP: *During the 1980s, the Holiday Bowl hosted many high scoring games. None was more exciting than the 1980 contest that featured Jim McMahon's last-second touchdown pass that enabled Brigham Young to defeat Southern Methodist 46–45.* BRIGHAM YOUNG UNIVERSITY

RIGHT: *Doug Flutie had plenty to celebrate when he completed a touchdown pass on the final play of the game to defeat Miami in 1984.* BOSTON COLLEGE

The game experienced many milestone events during the decade. In 1981, Alabama Coach Paul "Bear" Bryant surpassed Amos Alonzo Stagg on college football's all-time coaching win list with his 315th career victory.

His record would last four more years until it was surpassed in 1985 by Grambling's Eddie Robinson who achieved his 324th victory against Prairie View.

Coaching legend Joe Paterno won his second national title in 1986, holding on to defeat Miami in the Fiesta Bowl. Had the Hurricanes managed to pull out the last second victory, Miami would have added a fourth national championship to their 1980s total of three.

In 1982, the game experienced one of its more bizarre acts when California defeated Stanford on a final play that featured five laterals as the final ball carrier had to negotiate his way through the Stanford band. • • •

Paul "Bear" Bryant completed his coaching career in 1982. His final record included six national championships, twenty-two top-ten finishes, and a won-loss mark of 323–85–17. UNIVERSITY OF ALABAMA

Who's Number One

For a number of years, a large segment of college football coaches, administrators and fans were clamoring for a college football playoff. The situation became especially critical in the 1990s, as on three occasions, the two major polls could not agree on a national champion.

The nineties saw incremental steps to a format that would approach, yet not quite realize, a goal of determining the national championship on the field.

The first step was the Bowl Coalition of 1992–1994, which locked six conference champions and two at-large teams to four major bowls. From 1995–1997, the Bowl Alliance involved three bowls but eliminated automatic conference champion participation. As neither the Coalition or Alliance involved Big Ten or Pacific Ten teams, a national championship match-up between the nation's top two teams could not be guaranteed.

In 1998, the Bowl Championship

Eddie Robinson coached at Grambling for fifty-five seasons, a span that included eleven presidential administrations. When he retired after the 1997 season, he had a record of 408–165–15. GRAMBLING STATE UNIVERSITY

Series was formed that did include the Big Ten, the Pacific Ten, and the Rose Bowl. The BCS created a weekly ranking that involved a number of factors including polls, record, strength of schedule, and mathematical ratings formulas. The ratings were complicated to many fans and caused a great deal of controversy. They did however guarantee that the nation's number one and number two teams would meet in a championship contest.

Another change to college football in the 1990s was the birth of the "super conference." Conferences such as the Southeastern, Big 8, Western Athletic, and Mid-American expanded to include twelve or more teams. By expanding, these leagues were able to divide into divisions and hold conference championship games. The expanding leagues unfortunately resulted in the death of the Southwest Conference which was founded in 1914.

Joe Paterno won two national titles in the 1980s. Before taking the head job at Penn State in 1966, "Joe Pa" was a Nittany Lion assistant for 16 seasons. PENN STATE UNIVERSITY

Florida State coach Bobby Bowden won his 300th game with a victory over Clemson, coached by his son Tommy. FLORIDA STATE UNIVERSITY

Another change to the game was the elimination of tie games. Small colleges had instituted a tie-breaking procedure in 1981, with the major colleges adopting this rule in 1995.

The best teams of the 1990s were at Florida State and Nebraska. The Seminoles won two national titles, and as the decade ended, were in the midst of an unprecedented string of thirteen consecutive years finishing among the nation's top four teams. The Cornhuskers also won two championships and shared a third. Coach Tom Osborne called it a career in 1997 after 25 years as head coach.

Grambling's Eddie Robinson also retired in 1997 as college football's all-time win leader with 408 victories over 55 seasons in coaching.

College football in the 1990s was increasingly becoming an offensive

FACING PAGE: Nebraska's Tom Osborne finished his career at the top of his game. In his final five seasons he won three national titles and had a 60–3 record. UNIVERSITY OF NEBRASKA

game. Touchdowns, total offense, and scoring had never been higher.

As a result the ink was barely dry on individual and team records before they were surpassed. In 1998, Ricky Williams broke Tony Dorsett's 22-year old career rushing record only to see it surpassed the following year by Wisconsin's Ron Dayne.

However, those who toiled on defense finally gained notoriety. In 1997, Michigan's Charles Woodson became the first defensive player to win the Heisman Trophy, and numerous individual awards for defensive players were being created.

During his record-setting season, Ricky Williams dedicated many of his accomplishments to Doak Walker of SMU. Williams occasionally wore Walker's number 37 in tribute to the Hall of Famer who died during the 1998 season.
UNIVERSITY OF TEXAS

The shoes that traveled the last of 6,397 yards as Wisconsin's Ron Dayne surpassed the career rushing record of Ricky Williams are on display in the Record Breakers display.

LEFT: Charles Woodson catches a pass against Ohio State. His performance in this 1997 contest clinched the Heisman Trophy as he set up one touchdown on offense, scored another on a punt return, and prevented an Ohio State score with an interception in the end zone. UNIVERSITY OF MICHIGAN

BELOW: Florida's Danny Wuerffel set numerous major-college passing records, including career passing efficiency. UNIVERSITY OF FLORIDA

As college football entered the new century, the game had never been more popular. Despite the constrictions of athletic gender economics, schools were adding football to their athletic programs. Others were seeking to enter the ranks of the big time by elevating their programs to major college status. Most importantly, the game was receiving increased attention and attendance was at an all-time high of nearly 42 million tickets sold in 1999. • • •

Upon election to the Hall of Fame, a player or coach has a relief likeness placed in the museum's Hall of Champions.

CHAPTER III

The Museum

How the Museum Was Built

The College Football Hall of Fame opened in South Bend on August 25, 1995. The building and opening of the museum was the end of a three-year process when it was announced in June 1992 that the Hall of Fame would be relocated to South Bend from Kings Island, Ohio.

South Bend was selected by the National Football Foundation after requests for proposals were sent to the over 100 cities that sponsored a NFF chapter. From this request the foundation received 35 bids from which a field of five finalists emerged: South Bend, Houston, Atlanta, New Orleans, and the New Jersey Meadowlands.

South Bend was selected as the site for many factors that included the proximity to the city's convention center, and the tendency for similar halls of fame to thrive in small to medium size markets.

The building's unique design was made so that the building's exterior would look like that of a football stadium. As one enters the 100-yard circular ramp, he follows the 43-foot Pursuit of a Dream theme sculpture that represents a young player's journey from childhood idolatry of a football star through

The Grand Opening of the Hall of Fame in 1995 took place in conjunction with the annual Enshrinement Festival held each August.

Great Rivals

his travails in backyards, sand lots, and high school football fields before becoming a football hero in his own right.

The various sculptings throughout the museum are life-castings in which molds were taken of live models. In an interesting coincidence, the reliefs of the Hall of Fame members were crafted by a relative of Hall of Fame and Four Horsemen member Jim Crowley. Additionally, a relative of the legendary Pudge Heffelfinger worked on several of the museum's audio/visual elements.

Since the museum opened, it has won numerous local, regional, and national awards for design, audio/visual presentation, exhibitry, and overall presentation. • • •

All sports have intense rivalry games. However, college football rivalries may be the most passionate of all. Because of the fact that football rivals meet only once a season, the magnitude and importance of the game brings the intensity level of players and fans to heights not found in other sports.

The passionate fervor in which the games are played makes the emotional factor of determining a winner in these games ever important. For this reason, rivalry games are noted for their unpredictability.

Rivalries develop between teams largely due to geographic proximity, others become heated due to sustained battles over conference bragging rights, while a select few such as Army-Navy are national in scope. Nearly all of the great rivalries have been played for well over one hundred years.

The two dozen rivalries presented by the College Football Hall of Fame are just a sampling of these tradition-filled games. • • •

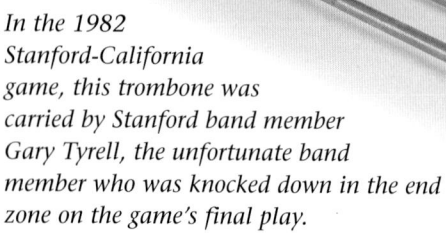

In the 1982 Stanford-California game, this trombone was carried by Stanford band member Gary Tyrell, the unfortunate band member who was knocked down in the end zone on the game's final play.

Covering the Game

The earliest public accounts of college football came in student publications and sporting magazines before the *New York Journal* introduced the first newspaper sports section in 1895.

Newspaper reporting was at its zenith during the 1920s when writers such as Grantland Rice, Damon Runyon, and others covered the game utilizing a wide range of literary elements including poetry.

During the 1920s, radio began covering the game on both the local and national levels, making national heroes out of otherwise regional celebrities.

Like radio, the advent of television initially was feared to have a detrimental effect of attendance. It quickly was learned that increased exposure led to a greater interest in the game, and increased admissions. Televised college football grew tremendously in the 1980s when cable networks began covering the game. Today's fan can view well over a half dozen games each Saturday with an occasional game often being televised during the mid-week. • • •

The typewriter, from which Grantland Rice wrote many of his columns, can be found in the Covering the Game display.

Fields, Footballs, and Officials

Where, with what, and how the rules of football have been judicated have changed greatly over the years.

The first games were played in open fields with spectators viewing the action by standing alongside the field, or from the lofty perch of a carriage or horseback. The first structures for seating were wooden stands before the first permanent concrete and steel stadium was built by Harvard in 1903.

Rule changes have greatly effected the size and markings of the field throughout the years. In the early part of the twentieth century one rule change created both longitudinal and latitudinal field markings from which the term gridiron was applied to football.

As intercollegiate football was first a kicking game, the ball was more like a soccer ball before the sport became a running game in the 1870s. Over time, the ball became more streamlined until 1934 when the ball took the shape it has today. • • •

The rules of 1903 called for field markings of both lateral and horizontal lines. As one rule stipulated that the quarterback proceed laterally five yards before turning up-field, the horizontal lines were used to aid officials.

Scholar-Athletes

Academic application, school leadership, citizenship, and football performance are the basic requirements to become recognized as a National Football Foundation scholar-athlete.

On both the local and national level the NFF recognizes a select few who live up to these high standards.

Since instituting the Scholar-Athlete program in 1959, over seven million dollars in scholarships have been awarded.

Past recipients have gone on to excel in a variety of fields including medicine, law, education, business, and the military. Those of note include the host of NBC's *Dateline*, Stone Phillips of Yale, and actors Mark Harmon of UCLA, and Utah State's Merlin Olsen. • • •

Before becoming a successful actor, Mark Harmon was a quarterback at UCLA. His father, Tom Harmon of Michigan, won the Heisman Trophy in 1940. NATIONAL BROADCASTING COMPANY

Evolution of the Equipment

As American football moved away from soccer and rugby and established itself as a unique sport, specialized equipment soon followed.

The first football specific equipment were shoes. Baseball spikes were first utilized with leather replacing the metal cleats. Cleat patterns were adapted for football, and over the years, the cleat material has changed to include wood, rubber, and plastic.

Today's shoes are made from a variety of materials and offer several various cleat patterns for specific positions and field conditions.

From the beginning of the game, of most obvious concern to the player, was the head and facial areas. The first piece of protective equipment was the nose guard. Made of hard rubber, the nose guard was held in place by the teeth and an elastic band around one's head.

The first helmet was developed in 1893 for Navy's Joe Reeves by an Annapolis shoemaker after a doctor warned Reeves that another kick to the head could result in his death. This crude helmet was replaced by the head harness, which was a combination of straps and pads that also covered the ears.

While helmet development grew to cover more of the head and included more padding, helmets still offered little protection as long as the helmet sat directly on the skull.

The development of the suspension helmet in 1917 allowed the head to be cradled away from the helmet's shell through a series of straps. These new helmets were ventilated, offering the player a small degree of comfort.

The next developments came in the construction materials of the helmet's shell, which went from leather, to the first plastic models in the early 1940s.

The player of 1900 had little protection besides a canvas vest and nose mask. Before the advent of helmets, many players simply wore long hair.

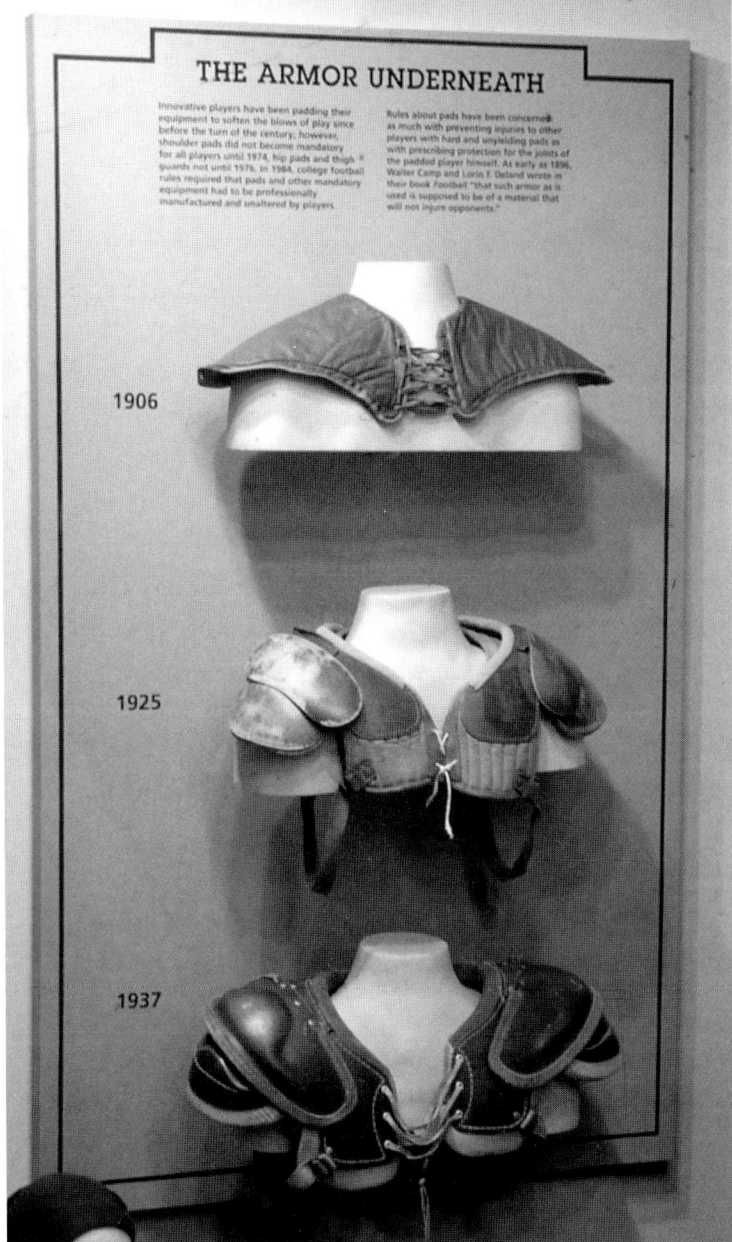

The Evolution of the Equipment display shows the evolution of uniforms, helmets, shoes, and shoulder pads.

In the past 30 years, the suspension design has been improved upon and altered to include air or water filled cells that could be adjusted to each player's specification.

Aside from the helmet, the most obvious piece of football equipment are pads, specifically shoulder pads. The first shoulder pads offered little protection as they were two pieces of lightly padded material that were worn over the shoulders. These grew into larger pieces that included thicker padding and hard leather plates.

In the 1930s, cantilever pads were developed to offer greater protection and absorb shock. Since the 1930s, position specific shoulder pads were developed and advancements have been made in stronger, lighter weight materials. • • •

Pigskin Pageantry

College football is much more than what happens between the lines. The traditional events and activities that happen before, during, and after the game, create an atmosphere that is not found at other sporting events.

The traditions of marching bands, fight songs, mascots, cheerleaders, tailgating, and homecoming originated with college football and are all nearly one hundred years old or older.

Even before the advent of the automobile, college football fans tailgated. In the days before stadiums, spectators often viewed the game from horse-drawn carriages set up alongside the field. Often times these fans brought food and drink to the game.

Team nicknames and mascots were also introduced early in collegiate football history. Perhaps the first known mascot was Yale's bulldog Handsome Dan who made his first appearance in 1889.

While many nicknames relate to animals, occupations, or other unique localized traits, many more schools utilize more generic images for their nicknames. The three most common college nicknames are Eagles, Tigers, and Cougars.

The first known cheerleaders were at the University of Minnesota in 1898. For the next thirty years this was a male-only sideline activity until Marquette introduced the first female cheerleader in 1927. • • •

At the turn of the twentieth century, students often went to the game in highly decorated carriages.

Bowl Games

The first bowl game was played on January 1, 1902 when Michigan was invited to Pasadena by the Tournament of Roses Committee to play Stanford. The Wolverines easily won the game 49–0. Due to the disparity in the score, football was not a part of the annual Pasadena New Year's Day festivities again until 1916.

Because of the national appeal of the sport, football became an annual part of the festivities.

The term "bowl game" originated when the Pasadena Tournament of Roses Committee built the Rose Bowl Stadium, which was patterned after the Yale Bowl.

The Rose Bowl remained the only post-season game until the mid 1930s when the cities of Miami, New Orleans, Dallas, and El Paso began staging New Year's Day games to promote their cities as tourist attractions.

With the exception of a few minor bowl games that came and went, the annual calendar contained only a half dozen or so bowl games until the 1970s. In 1980, the figure had grown to thirteen bowl games, with the figure now approaching twice that number.

During the 1980s, sponsors began to add their names to bowl titles, making for the many different sounding bowl games of the present. The history of post-season play shows some interesting and entertaining bowl names. Some of the long forgotten small college bowls include the Bean Bowl, the Boot Hill Bowl, the Cement Bowl, the Cigar Bowl, and the Kickapoo Bowl.

The past decade has seen the bowl picture change because of the formation of the Bowl Coalition, Bowl Alliance, and Bowl Championship Series. In addition, most bowls have developed predetermined conference tie-ins that assign bowl bids. • • •

The Bowl Exhibit contains trophies and memorabilia from the most recent bowl games.

National Champions

With the exception of the small school ranks, major college football has been the one sport in the United States that has never had a game or series of games determine an undisputed national champion.

The first attempts at naming a national champion came in the mid 1920s from mathematic rating services that judged team performance according to various objective formulas and factors. Several of these rating systems then applied their formulas to the results of previous seasons to pre-date national champions. Most of the early mathematic polls have been replaced by computer generated rating formulas.

The MacArthur Bowl resembles a football stadium complete with goal posts, yard lines, and rows of seats. On the exterior of the trophy are carved the names of all the trophy's recipients.

In 1936, the Associated Press created the first weekly poll of sportswriters. The United Press then instituted a poll in 1950 that was voted on by a group of coaches. Both polls are still in existence today, with the coaches poll now being sponsored by *USA Today* and ESPN.

The National Football Foundation began awarding the MacArthur Bowl to its national champion in 1959. The trophy was the gift of an anonymous donor in the name of General Douglas MacArthur. The bowl is made of four hundred ounces of silver and was designed by Tiffany & Company, using suggestions made by MacArthur.

Having more than one board vote on the national champion has resulted in numerous instances where the polls could not agree on a national champion. There has also been the problem that from 1965 until the mid 1970s, some of the polls determined a champion before the bowl games and some did not make a selection until after the bowl games were played.

Small college championships have not had the colorful and controversial history of the major college football championships. There was little formal recognition of the best of the small schools until the major wire services began issuing small college polls in the late 1950s.

When the NCAA broke small college football into divisional play in 1973, they also began a series of playoff games that determined the national championship outcome on the field, a practice that the NAIA has done since 1956. • • •

Pantheon

Aside from the annual All-America selections that began in 1889, college football did not honor individual players until 1935. That year the Downtown Athletic Club of New York awarded the DAC Trophy to Chicago's Jay Berwanger as the best collegiate player east of the Mississippi. A year later the award became a national honor and was renamed the Heisman Memorial Trophy to honor the former coach and DAC athletic director.

In 1937, the Maxwell Memorial Club of Philadelphia also began to name a nation's best player through the granting of the Maxwell Award.

As backs and ends dominated these awards, the Football Writers Association began to honor the nation's best interior lineman in 1946 with the Outland Award.

The eighties and nineties have witnessed an explosion of these awards as athletic clubs and service groups around the nation have instituted trophies to honor players in a wide range of individual positions.

The Pantheon is an exhibit which features the most notable of these awards. • • •

The Pantheon contains all the major individual awards and trophies as well as the jersey of the game's top players from the most recent season.

Award	Description	Year
Heisman Trophy	Outstanding player	1935
Maxwell Award	Outstanding player	1937
Outland Trophy	Outstanding interior lineman	1946
Camp Award	Outstanding player	1967
Lombardi Award	Outstanding lineman	1970
O'Brien Award	Best quarterback	1981
Butkus Award	Best linebacker	1985
Thorpe Award	Best defensive back	1986
Walker Award	Best running back	1990
Nagurski Award	Best defensive player	1993

Hall of Honor

The National Football Foundation and College Hall of Fame annually honors individuals who have contributed to our society and amateur football through several major awards.

The highest honor given by the National Football Foundation is the Gold Medal Award, which was first presented in 1958 to President Dwight Eisenhower. Since that first award, numerous other presidents, elected officials, and captains of industry have been honored for bringing into their professional lives the fundamental values taught in amateur sport.

Other major awards presented by the NFF are the Distinguished American Award and the Award for Outstanding Contribution to Amateur Football. The recipients of these awards must have exhibited leadership and made a significant contribution to amateur football. The NFF also honors a football official and an athletic director. • • •

President Dwight Eisenhower received the first Gold Medal presented by the NFF at its first annual dinner in 1958. NATIONAL FOOTBALL FOUNDATION

How One Becomes a Hall of Famer

There are several criteria one must meet before being considered for election to the College Football Hall of Fame.

Nominations of players and coaches may be made by any National Football Foundation member as well as by member universities. A player must have been recognized as a major first team All-America, have played his last collegiate game at least ten years previously, be retired from the professional game, and proven himself worthy as a citizen after his playing career.

A coach becomes eligible three years after retirement. He must have coached at least ten years and have won over 60 percent of his games.

Once a player or coach is nominated, his eligibility is verified before his name is sent to one of several regional review committees. These committees review the candidates from their geographic area and pass on their recommendation to be included on the national ballot. The nominations placed on the ballot are then reviewed by an Honors Court of twelve former coaches, players, athletic directors, administrators and media members to determine each year's class of inductees.

In 1996, the National Football Foundation began electing players and coaches who participated below the Division I-A level. These players are subject to the same standards as major college players and coaches. • • •

These segments are parts of two murals that dominate the entry hall to the College Football Hall of Fame. The segment on the right depicts Navy's Roger Staubach, Grambling's Eddie Robinson and Ohio State's Woody Hayes.

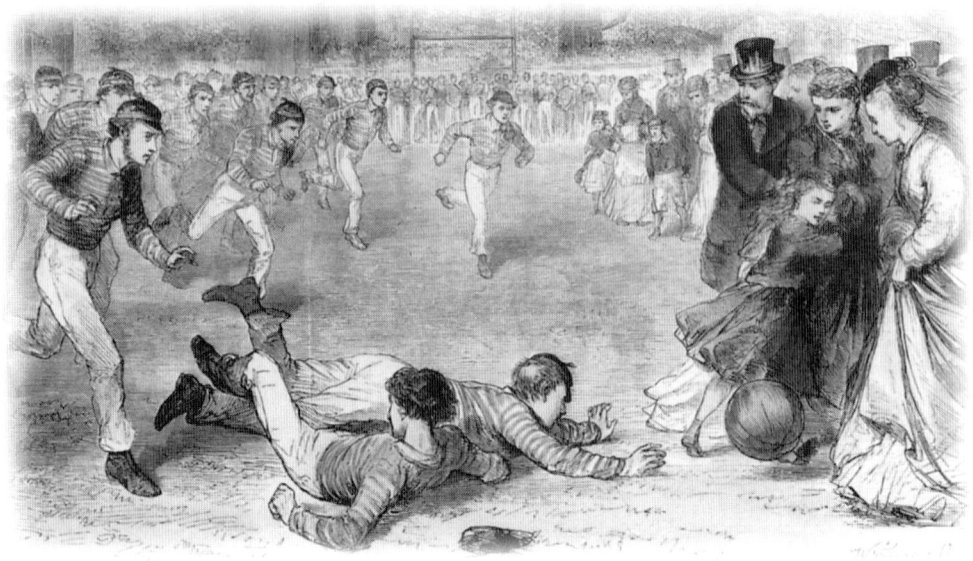

ABOUT THE AUTHOR

Before he was ever born, Kent Stephens has had a link to college football. While watching the 1953 Rose Bowl, Kent's parents noticed the name of Wisconsin end Kent Peters. Liking the name, they remembered it in July of that year when Kent was born.

Oddly, Kent's niece Kristen has a similar story in being named after the Queen of the Rose Parade.

Kent is one of the lucky sports fans who has been able to turn a life long passion into a career. While he has an encyclopedic knowledge of college football, his first love is college basketball. Kent grew up in Cincinnati following the exploits of the Cincinnati Bearcats who appeared in five consecutive Final Fours from 1959–1963.

He has a broadcasting degree from the University of Cincinnati and a Masters in Sports Management from the Ohio State University.

He resides in Elkhart, Ind. with his wife Valerie and their dog, Maddie.